Merry Christmas 2016.
Dear Christopher

Ways into Science

All about Plants

Love,
Grandmaman
XXX

Peter Riley

W

FRANKLIN WATTS
LONDON • SYDNEY

Franklin Watts
Published in Great Britain in 2016
by The Watts Publishing Group

Copyright images © Franklin Watts 2014
Copyright text © Peter Riley 2014
(Text has previously appeared in Ways into Science:
Growing Plants (2003) but has been comprehensively
re-written for this edition.)

Editor: Julia Bird
Designer: Basement 68

ISBN: 978 1 4451 3470 3
Dewey classification number: 580

Printed in China

FSC
www.fsc.org
MIX
Paper from
responsible sources
FSC® C104740

Franklin Watts
An imprint of
Hachette Children's Group
Part of The Watts Publishing Group
Carmelite House
50 Victoria Embankment
London EC4Y 0DZ

An Hachette UK Company
www.hachette.co.uk
www.franklinwatts.co.uk

Photo acknowledgements: Moller/Watts except: Dreamstime/
Rogério Bernardo: 21tc. Maksym Gorpenyuk: 13l. Richard
Griffin: 5t, 8, 17t, 17bl, 17cr. Péter Gudella 21bl. Arina P
Habich: 3, 9b. Jojjik: 15tl. Kosmos111: 16bl. Maksim Masalski:
13tr. Verena Matthew: 15tr. David Morrison: 5c, 10b.
Motorolka: 14cr. Photogenes: 6, 28b. Puchan: 7. Rigmanyi:
4, 24. Rwb: 14bl. Eugene Sergeev: 5cb, 9t. Sters: 15bl. Wolgin:
16tr. Shutterstock/SeDmi: front cover b.

Every attempt has been made to clear copyright.
Should there be any inadvertent omission,
please apply to the Publishers for rectification.

Contents

All **sorts** of **plants**

There are all sorts of plants. Many plants grow flowers that have bright colours. Trees and bushes are plants that are woody.

Point to the trees, bushes and flowers in this garden.

Plants grow in wild places, too.

Look at this picture. What plants can you see growing next to the path, in the field and in the forest?

The **parts** of a **plant**

Here are the parts of a plant that has flowers.

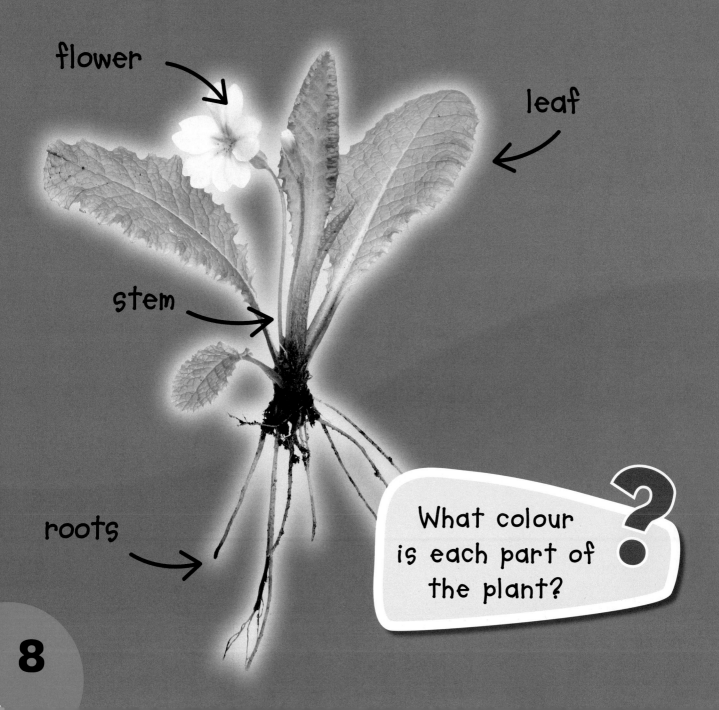

flower

leaf

stem

roots

What colour is each part of the plant?

8

Some plants do not have flowers.

Some trees have cones instead of flowers.

Which part of these plants is in the ground? Turn the page to find out.

Roots

Roots grow underground. They take up water from the soil.

Roots help to hold plants in the soil. This tree has thick, woody roots.

This plant has been growing in a pot for a long time. The root has grown round and round inside the pot. It is 'pot bound'.

The plant must be put into a larger pot. This is called repotting.

Which part of the plant grows from the root? Turn the page to find out.

Stems

The stem grows from the root. It holds up the leaves and the flowers. Some plants only have one stem.

Some plants have lots.

Some plants have stems that are hidden by leaves.

A tree has a woody stem called a trunk. It is covered in bark.

Every year, a tree makes a new ring of wood in its trunk. Do you think this tree is older or younger than you?

What grows on a stem? Turn the page to find out.

Leaves

Leaves grow on a stem. They are different shapes, colours and sizes.

Some trees lose all their leaves in the autumn and grow new ones in the spring.

Other trees keep their leaves all year round.

Flowers

Some plants have lots of little flowers.

Some plants have one large flower.

The coloured parts of a flower are called the petals.

How many petals has this flower got?

What forms inside flowers? Turn the page to find out.

Seeds

Seeds form inside flowers. Seeds grow into flowering plants.

Some seeds grow in fruits. They are called pips.

pips

seeds

Some seeds grow in pods.

Bulbs

Some plants have short stems and store food in their leaves. This makes them swell up and form a bulb.

The bulbs are planted in soil.

The food in the bulb helps the leaves and flowers grow.

Planting **seeds**

Laura and Sam are planting seeds.

They put
soil into pots.

They make
four holes.

They put a seed
in each hole.

They cover the
seeds with soil.

Sam waters his seeds.

Laura does not water her seeds.

What do you think will happen after a few days? Turn the page to find out.

Seedlings

Sam's seeds have grown stems and roots. They are called seedlings.

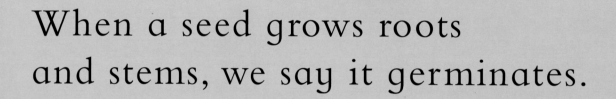

When a seed grows roots and stems, we say it germinates.

Laura's seeds have not grown roots or a stem.

Why do you think the seeds have not germinated?

Plants and light

Nicole and Matthew have cress seedlings.

Nicole puts her seedlings in a place with plenty of light.

Matthew puts his seedlings in a dark place.

What do you think will happen in a few days? Turn the page to find out.

Light tests

Nicole's seedlings have grown into plants with dark green leaves and short, firm stems.

Matthew's seedlings have grown into plants with pale leaves and long, weak stems.

Try this test with some other kinds of seedling. What do you find?

22

Sam sets up a test to see if plants grow towards the light.

This cover has a hole cut in one side. →

He leaves the cover over the plants for a few days. This is how they look.

What does Sam's test show?

Plants and warmth

Plants need warmth to grow well. A greenhouse traps the heat from the Sun. This makes it warm inside the greenhouse. Plants grow well there.

Jess is comparing how cress seedlings grow.

She turns a plastic cup upside down to make a mini greenhouse. She puts it on pot A.

Pot A   Pot B

Which seedlings do you think will grow faster? Can you explain why?

We grow plants for food. Which parts of plants do we eat? Turn the page to find out.

Plants we eat

Most of our food comes from plants.

We eat the flowers and stems of the broccoli plant.

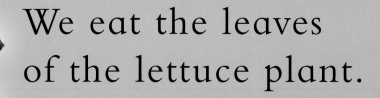

We eat the leaves of the lettuce plant.

Oranges are the fruit of orange trees.

Carrots are roots from carrot plants.

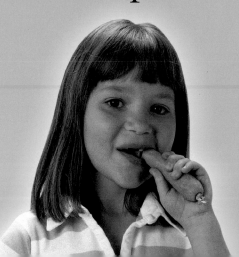

Peas are the seeds of the pea plant.

Bread is made from the seeds of the wheat plant.

Make a chart like this and find out which part of the plant people eat.

	Root	Leaf	Stem	Flower	Seed	Fruit
Turnip	✓	✗	✗	✗	✗	✗
Apple tree	?	?	?	?	?	?
Tomato plant	?	?	?	?	?	?
Cabbage	?	?	?	?	?	?
Sunflower	?	?	?	?	?	?

Useful words

bark – the covering on a tree.

bulb – a ball-shaped object with a short stem. Its leaves are swollen with food. It is planted in the soil and grows roots, leaves and flowers.

flower – the parts of the plant where seeds are made. Flowers come in all shapes, sizes and colours.

fruit – the part of the plant that contains its seeds and is often eaten.

germinate – when a seed germinates it grows a stem and roots, which can eventually grow into a full plant.

leaf – a flat, usually green, part of a plant that grows from the stem.

pip – the name for the seed of a flower when it grows in the middle of the fruit.

root – the part of the plant that grows down into the soil to collect water. It also holds the plant firmly in the soil.

seed – the part of a fruit which has a tiny plant and its store of food inside it.

seedling – a young plant that has just started to grow from the seed.

stem – the part of a plant which is usually long and thin. Roots grow from the stem under the ground, and leaves grow from the stem above ground.

trunk – the thick stem of a tree.

Some answers

Here are some answers to the questions we have asked in this book. Don't worry if you had some different answers to ours: you may be right, too. Talk through your answers with other people and see if you can explain why they are right.

Page 7 Small plants with yellow flowers next to the path, grass in the field, trees in the forest.

Page 8 Flowers – yellow; stem – pink; leaves – green; roots – white.

Page 13 The tree trunk has more than 30 rings, which means the tree is more than 30 years old.

Page 15 The flower has got five petals.

Page 20 The seeds have not germinated because they did not have any water.

Page 23 Sam's test shows that plants grow towards the light.

Page 25 The seedlings in pot A will grow better because of the warmth created by the cup acting as a greenhouse.

Page 27 We eat: turnip – root; apple tree – fruit; tomato plant – fruit; (NB Only the fruit of the tomato plant is edible. Other parts are poisonous.) sunflower – seed; cabbage – leaves.

Index

About this book

Ways into Science is designed to encourage children to think about their everyday world in a scientific way and to make investigations to test their ideas. There are five lines of enquiry that scientists make in investigations. These are grouping and classifying, observing over time, making a fair test, searching for patterns and researching using secondary sources.

• When children open this book they are already making one line of enquiry – researching about plants. As they read through the book they are invited to make other lines of enquiry and to develop skills in scientific investigation.

• On pages 6, 7, 8 ,13 and 15 they are invited to try out their observational skills.

• On pages 19 and 21 they are asked to predict the results of fair tests where observations are made over time.

• On page 22 they are challenged to make their own investigation from what they have read, involving a fair test where observations are made over time.

• On pages 20, 23 and 25 they are asked to draw conclusions from investigations.

• On page 27 they are asked to make a table and fill it in by classifying the edible parts of plants using knowledge acquired by reading earlier parts of the book.